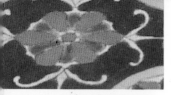

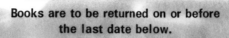

**Books are to be returned on or before
the last date below.**

2 9 OCT 2003

ITHDRAWN

LIBREX—

South Beach Style

By Laura Cerwinske

Photography by Steven Brooke

Design by Barry Zaid

Preface by Bernard Zyscovich, AIA

Harry N. Abrams, Inc., Publishers

Library of Congress Cataloging-in-Publication Data

Cerwinske, Laura.
  South Beach style / by Laura Cerwinske ; Photography by Steven Brooke ;
Foreword by Bernard Zyscovich ; Design by Barry Zaid.
      p. cm.
      ISBN 0-8109-9080-6
1. Architecture – Florida – Miami Beach – 20th century.
2. South Beach (Miami Beach, Fla.) – Buildings, structures, etc.
3. Miami Beach (Fla.) – Buildings, structures, etc. 4. Art Deco Historic
District (Miami Beach, Fla.) 5. Interior decoration – Florida – Miami
Beach – History – 20th century. 6. Decoration and ornament – Florida –
Miami Beach – Art deco.
I. Brooke, Steven. II. Title.

NA735.M4 C476 2002
720'.9759'381 — dc21

2002005829

South Beach Style was produced by Laura Cerwinske
Editorial Production, Miami, Florida

Copyright © 2002 Laura Cerwinske
Photographs copyright © 2002 Steven Brooke

*Sustainable Hedonism: The South Beach Formula for Urban
Vitality* copyright © 2002 Bernard Zyscovich and Laura
Cerwinske

Published in 2002 by Harry N. Abrams, Incorporated,
New York All rights reserved. No part of the contents
of this book may be reproduced without the written
permission of the publisher

Production Manager: Alyn Evans

Printed and bound in Italy
10 9 8 7 6 5 4 3 2 1

Harry N. Abrams, Inc.
100 Fifth Avenue
New York, N.Y. 10011
www.abramsbooks.com

Abrams is a subsidiary of

Dedication

For Evie and Bob, whose
romance began on Miami Beach.
For Jona, our tower of creativity,
whose recognition of South Beach
as a resource has nourished his art
and propelled his career.
L.C.

For Suzanne and Miles
S.B.

For Audrey, Alina, and Silvester
B.Z.

Acknowledgments

Our deep gratitude to graphic
designers Julie and Barry Harley
for their great skill, personalities,
and professionalism.

Contents

Preface

Sustainable Hedonism:
The South Beach Formula
for Urban Vitality

By Bernard Zyscovich, AIA

Urban energy is sexual—exciting, provocative,
unpredictable. Vital cities, in their perpetual
compression, integration, and reconfiguration,
are possessed of limitless sources of pleasure
and danger. Moreover, they promote self-
expression. Self-conscious and voyeuristic, they
are hotbeds of fashion, art, and exhibitionism,
places to see and be seen in. Vital cities are up
all night.

   Think Berlin in the 1920s. Paris in the Fifties.
Tokyo in the Eighties. Barcelona in the Nineties.
New York and Rome eternally. And South Beach
since its renaissance twenty years ago. Each
embodies or embodied a collision of social,
religious, ethnic, political, and sexual cultures

The Lincoln Cinemas, the landmark entry
to the country's first pedestrian mall, Lincoln Road.

and age groups. Each was or is creating community within a state of constant flux.

While the so called "New Urbanism" would have us believe that urban vitality is generated by a specific type of programmatic development, the truth is virtually antithetical: the requisite sexual pulse of urban excitement derives from the conscious embrace of chaos as entertainment and of density as nourishment. Vital cities evolve layer by layer and change hour by hour.

South Beach, as a mecca for art, fashion, and sexual expression, exemplifies the viability of Sustainable Hedonism more than any other city in America, perhaps in the Western world. It is simultaneously historic and contemporary, local and international, touristic and residential, seasonal and perpetual. Yet underlying this dynamic of contradictions and orientations, it is the city's hedonistic appeal—of sun, sea, flesh, and flash—that catalyzes its vitality.

From Club Culture to Cafe Society

What makes South Beach so urbanistically relevant today is that its hedonistic qualities are what America is seeking everywhere— from the workplace to the gym, from the amusement park to the shopping mall. In South Beach,

A weekend flea market and farmers' market on Lincoln Road.

socializing, shopping, entertainment, and a convenient workout are all at hand. It is a one-stop escape without leaving the neighborhood.

Americans have learned that life doesn't have to be differentiated according to seasons, time zones, or stages in order to partake of diversion. We don't have to wait for a raise or a vacation or retirement to have a variety of pleasures available at every moment. No one embraced this fusion of entertainment and work more than the dot-com entrepreneurs. Adapting their offices into adult playgrounds, they became workaholic hedonists, filling more-than-twelve-hour-long workdays with recreation as intense—and as available—as their labors. Combine yuppie drive and hippie indulgence with dot-com ingenuity, and Dionysian Calvinism is born.

The transposition of this philosophy from the office to the street is the true form of contemporary urban vitality. Picture adaptive reuse and urban mixed use in overdrive and you have South Beach, where gyms, clubs, beaches, and sidewalks host a continual parade of nubile skin and gay flamboyance. At virtually any hour, you can have the makings of a fabulous body—or at least the sight of one—within a stone's throw in any given direction.

The theater of the street: eating, drinking, skateboarding, and socializing on Ocean Drive.

The Opposite of Greenfield Development

For those who built and frequented early Miami Beach, pleasure was a destination, dreamed of and planned for, but certainly not a perpetual way of life. A seaside escape for the Jewish middle class, it was a place to bathe in the ocean, go to the theater, and socialize with friends who also came seeking respite from the gray north. Once "the season" was over, however, you went back home—and to work. For those of today's generation who don't want to be limited as to when and where they work, the urban vitality of a place such as South Beach makes "all the world a stage"—an office, a playground, a trysting spot. South Beach is Puritanism's fallen frontier; furthermore, it is the living, growing, gritty manifestation of everything to which the New Urbanism merely aspires. South Beach is the lusty face of the true urban future.

Sustainable Hedonism, spiritually descended from the Sixties consciousness, expresses the urban imprint of indulgent former hippies who, having known hallucination, are unwilling to live life without fantasy. Where better than a sandbar whose architecture was developed as stagecraft as a place to act out a generation's fear of ennui? And who better to pave the way than the generation that had grown bored with the blandness and security of

Historic Espanola Way, built as a locale for adult entertainment by the owner of a large Mediterranean-style resort hotel. Desi Arnaz played "Babalu" here.

the Fifties, traveled the world, experienced the thrill of redefining life, and understood idealism? If the 1980s was about the resurgence of pleasure seeking, it was the children of the Sixties who opened the disco doors—and who pointed the way to South Beach's revitalization.

From its very inception, the development of Miami Beach has been more about fulfillment of the subconscious than creation of the material. Its architecture, drawn from cinematographic, industrial, and nautical design, is exactly what you think Art Deco architecture would be in such a place. However, while streamlined in appearance, the style makes little sense in reality, for the buildings are neither machines nor ships nor stage sets. Their thinly veneered façades are plays on the wistful dreams of movie images and the futuristic.

Totally nonprogrammatic, Tropical Deco architecture is static in comparison to the power of its illusion. Compared with its stylistic contemporaries—modern, Victorian, shingle style, classical—the Art Deco architecture of Miami Beach is literally superficial, its Art Deco–ness occurring purely on the surface. And unlike the Art Deco architecture of other parts of the world, its richness does not occur in the differentiation of materials—there are no aluminum or brass inlays and few glass mosaics. Totally economical, the stylistic effects are all created in stucco and extend only as far as the lobby. From its inception, therefore, the built environment of South Beach—simple, inexpensive, and decorative—has been stagecraft.

While the architectural concentration of the historically designated, one-square-mile Art Deco district was built, essentially, at the same time (the decade of the 1930s), it is important to note that it was also erected one building at a time, in a sequence based on patterns that were driven by a slow and methodical evolution of what was important—economically conveying tropical resort and seasonal life. Even though the style's consistency is largely a result of its simultanaeity and uniform lot size and setbacks, it is also the product of a number of like minds. The architects and builders of the Tropical Deco form were all intent on applying the most romantic and captivating imagery of the time. Nevertheless, the unity of style is a virtual phenomenon, a case in which the environment appears to be the product almost of one mind. Who really were these guys and how did this happen? Did they meet together, smoke cigars, and have a secret handshake? We know their names and something of their histories, but how is it that they decided, individually and in concert, that working in this one style would be so interesting?

Not Just a Pretty Face

Today these facades have become layers of surfaces and textures, revealing sixty years of social history. When the revival movement for the

restoration (and designation) of the district began in the late 1970s, it was, once more, the superficial that served as a bold statement.

In 1982 designer Leonard Horowitz painted a rainbow of pastel hues on the exterior of the venerable Friedman's Bakery, where nearly all the Beach community converged on Friday afternoons for their Shabbat challahs. Leonard, whose family came to the Beach from New York every year for six months during the entire course of his childhood, articulated the layers of color and detailing in a way that made the building appear confectionery (ideal, of course, for a bakery). More than simply the color itself, it was also the way he treated the color—like cake frosting—that contradicted the impression of the building's solidity and that of the others whose new palettes followed. Originally white, the buildings' surface textures changed with the effects of light, evoking the impression of carving or bas-relief. The confectionery colors, on the other hand, inverted traditional expectations of a building, creating a sort of anti-architecture.

Architects want to convey a building's weight and rootedness to the ground. We're interested in the material and its relationship to the form and how the structure meets the street. Leonard's palette, however, made the buildings look like petit- fours. His use of color abstracted them, objectified them, made them look weightless. And it

Shopping along the western end of Lincoln Road.

was this weightless effect that gave the buildings so magical a look in photographs. In one fell swoop, the Tropical Deco architecture of Miami Beach gained a new career—architecture as fashion accessory.

The color-generated rebirth of the Art Deco district was a revelation—an architectural coming out. Like the population that embraced the district, the architecture itself seemingly transformed from straight to gay. The buildings, no longer weighted by the depressing modernist browns and beiges imposed on them in the 1970s, suddenly exhibited pride in their decorative quality. Gay pride and Deco pride. Gay liberation and architectural liberation. In Miami Beach the two movements became synonymous.

From the Lay-Away Plan to Planning to Get Laid; From Pay as You Go to Play as You Go

The irony of this social evolution lies again in South Beach's origins. Founded by and for the Jewish middle class, which was excluded from other American resorts, the community's population was as homogeneous as its architecture. This and the subsequent generations of the 1940s and Fifties were survivors of the Depression. They knew what hardship meant and were willing to work and sacrifice for their leisure reward. They lived on the lay-away plan, paying installments for the deferred pleasures of their day in the sun.

The east side of the island— Washington Avenue, Collins Avenue, and Ocean Drive—was then, like today, mainly touristic, dense with hotels and shops. Easy accessibility to social acitivity and to the beach was accommodated by ground-floor lobbies, verandas, and porches. The sidewalk was the community "living room," the stage on which the theater of life could be observed and where promenades brought people together. From Washington Avenue west, the island was predominantly residential. While providing less mixed-use activity, it was nevertheless also designed for pedestrian friendliness, its buildings sharing the same stylistic treatments. The cross streets like Lincoln Road bridged the divide between east and west. Today, this remains the basic pattern of the city; it is the philosophy of life and the vast need to accommodate cars that have changed.

The most pressing issue for South Beach today, aside from parking, is how to sustain the social qualities and creative energy that have marked it from its inception while promoting its growth as an urban nexus. The answer is fundamental: by bringing arts and culture to the center of life and green to where there is now concrete.

OVERLEAF The culmination of the north axis of Ocean Drive at 15th Street, a counterpoint in forms, a new kind of "frozen music."

21

Introduction

The Architectural History and Cultural Evolution of South Beach

South Beach is an international playground and urban neighborhood in one. Created from swampland and conceived for fun and profit, it has metamorphosed over the decades from speculator's dream to photographer's fantasy. Once almost exclusively a haven for the retired, it is today as much a home to the restless (artists and fashion professionals) and the relocated (South Americans and Europeans). Street savvy meets sophistication in South Beach's countless clubs. Its street chic combines a Caribbean flavor with the cosmopolitan. A mecca for gays and tourists, it has a casual, colorful, and sensuous manner of living that promotes perpetual reinvention.

Palm Garden at 752 Meridian Avenue, designed by
H. H. Mundy, 1923.

In architecture, interior design, graphic design, fashion, and food, the South Beach style signals both a collusion and collision of sensibilities. Like its natural and urban setting, it celebrates eclecticism and exaggeration. It fuses resort and urban sensibilities along with gay, straight, androgynous, and as-yet-unnamed sexualities. It merges the serene with the kinetic and the distinctly local with the international.

The source of this continually transforming and self-renewing energy is the concentration of creative people who reside, visit, and come to work in South Beach. Their expression is evident everywhere: in the way they dress, dine, party, work, and design and furnish their homes. Whether stripped-down and streamlined or lavish and ornate, whether exotically exuberant or tropically refined, the South Beach style exudes a passion for the creative. This book is a celebration of that creativity.

While today South Beach is one of the world's most celebrated resorts, as recently as the turn of the 1900s, it was little more than a three-block-wide sandbar—uninhabited, mosquito-ridden, and separated from the fledgling town of Miami by an impenetrable swamp. The Beach's official history began in 1868 when a New Jerseyan named John Lum, on his way north from Havana by steamer, spotted a stand of coconut palms. Envisioning a coconut plantation, he set out to find investors and eventually purchased

the island for thirty-five cents an acre.

Lum's choice of location was brilliant. His choice of crops, however, proved disastrous. Infertile soil and blight ruined the palms, while vast mosquito infestations made work on the sandbar impossible. By 1890 Lum had said "nuts" to the coconuts, and the narrow strip of island beach was again deserted.

Nearly twenty years later, John Collins, a New Jersey horticulturist who had been one of Lum's investors, came south on the new Florida East Coast Railway to take a look at his failed $5,000 venture. As he surveyed the remains of the Lum plantation, he too had a vision: avocados.

Collins planted the Lum site with varieties that fruited all year round. He found himself with a bumper crop, but, unfortunately, no economical means of transporting it. Hence, his second vision: a canal and bridge connecting the island to mainland Miami and the railroad. Collins pioneered the project but ran out of funds before its completion. The two brothers who had financed it, bankers John and James Lummus, bought out Collins and had a vision of their own: "Fairy Land," a bathhouse on the ocean side of the island that would lure the tourists flocking south on the new railway. With no completed bridge, it would be reached by a twenty-five-cent ferry from the mainland. The ferry ride to Fairy Land made the

Spanish romanticism is enhanced by a sensitive color palette on an apartment building on the 1300 block of Meridian Avenue.

little beach off mainland Miami an official resort destination.

Enter Miami Beach's next champion—Carl Fisher, creator of the Indianapolis Speedway and the first marketer of the automobile headlight. While boating around Biscayne Bay during a visit to his winter home in Miami, he noticed the unfinished bridge. He thought about Fairy Land at the island's south end and the avocado farm at the north, and yet another vision emerged. Fisher called his "The American Riviera."

Fisher provided Collins with the funds to complete his bridge in exchange for the land adjacent to the Lummus brothers' property. Then, in partnership with the Lummuses, he began clearing swamps and filling in land. Black laborers from Mississippi and the Bahamas hacked out the dense mangroves. Huge dredging equipment, fueled by burning mangrove wood, scooped sand from the bay bottom to cover and extend the giant sandbar. The dredging went on day and night for a year and half at a cost of $52,000 a day. Once the land had settled to an even four feet above sea level, topsoil from the Everglades was brought in to cover it, and Bermuda grass was planted by hand. Finally, exotic tropical trees were imported to line the island's new streets.

The dredging had widened the narrow sandbar by nine blocks and

The Hotel Webster at 1220 Collins Avenue was designed by Henry Hohauser, 1936.

created channels deep enough for yachts to dock at the waterfront. In 1913 Collins completed his bridge, and Carl Fisher broke ground for his first grand hotel, the Flamingo. It would have an eleven-story glass-domed illuminated tower. He was determined to make Miami Beach "a city like Magic, like the romantic places you read and dream about, but never get to see."

Fisher built a new winter house for himself on the island and plotted out a shopping street that would connect the bay and the ocean. Called Lincoln Road, it was soon to be known as "The Fifth Avenue of the South." Visitors would alight from their yachts to view the windows of Saks and Bonwit Teller. Guests from the Flamingo, dressed in jewels and top hats, compared the latest fashions.

Vacationers and potential land buyers flocked to the new resort, where it was summer all winter long. By 1921 Miami Beach had five hotels. The lavish Roney Plaza, designed by New York architects Schultze and Weaver (who also designed Manhattan's Plaza Hotel and Coral Gables' Biltmore Hotel) opened in 1924. The hotels were so packed that visitors sometimes slept in parks.

Real estate speculators were making fortunes. John Collins and Carl Fisher, however, remained conservative in their sales, determined to keep their property, at the northern part of the island,

The Marlin hotel at 1225 Collins Avenue. Photograph by Carlos Domenech.

exclusive. They demanded high down payments, marketed toward wealthy mid-Westerners, and forbade sales of their land to Jews. The Lummus brothers, on the other hand, targeted middle-class, primarily Jewish buyers from New York and New Jersey who were eager to escape the gloom of northern winters and, eventually, of the Great Depression. Their property lay primarily below what is now Fifth Street.

From the 1920s through the 1930s, the building boom on Miami Beach produced a small treasury of Mediterranean-style hotels and apartments along with the greatest concentration of Art Deco architecture in the world. While the Mediterranean-style buildings incorporated some of the structural devices used in the hot climates of southern Italy, Spain, and North Africa, they were far more embracing of the region's romantic effects: thick plaster walls, barrel-tiled roofs, sculpted heraldry over windows and doors, and colorful glazed tiles and mosaics.

The more than 500 Art Deco buildings built almost entirely during the decade of the 1930s addressed that epoch's rapture with travel (the car, the ocean liner, the locomotive), industrialism, Hollywood glamour, and the exoticism of Latin culture. The tropical interpretation of Art Deco, for which I coined the term *Tropical Deco* in my first book on the area in 1981, shared many of the compositional elements intrinsic to Moderne design and to European and American "Big

ABOVE LEFT Friedman's Bakery as painted by Leonard Horowitz and as it appeared on the historic *Progressive Architecture* cover in the 1980s. **ABOVE RIGHT** The Ambassador at Meridian and 10th Street. **BELOW LEFT AND RIGHT** Cast friezes of Parisian Art Deco floral motifs contrast with German Bauhaus geometry.

35

City" Deco: combinations of flat and curved walls; extended parapets; concrete eyebrows shading rectangular and faceted corner windows; circular or porthole windows rectangularly framed; and lavish ornamentation, including friezes, reliefs, door surrounds, and finials.

The Tropical Deco architecture of what is now known as South Beach bears an aesthetic that is rare in today's urban landscape—consistency in design and scale as well as animation and harmony of geometry and decoration. It is an architecture created to evoke feelings of delight and planned to advantageously combine extremely modest construction costs with a popular, romantic, and modern appearance.

This is the South Beach that my mother, Evelyn Schwartz, née Auslander, grew up in, relocated from New York at the age of eleven, and where she met my father, Bob Schwartz. An animator with the Fleischer Studios, creators of Betty Boop, Popeye, and other great cartoon epics of the period, he had moved with the studio from New York to Miami in 1935. Their courtship was a purely Miami Beach affair.

The principal architects of Miami Beach's Art Deco community were Albert Anis, L. Murray Dixon, Roy F. France, Henry Hohauser, and Anton Skislewicz. Their origins ranged from Eastern Europe to the Midwest, and from New York to Florida. Most did not have, or did not complete, a formal

The soaring finial of the Breakwater Hotel at 940 Ocean Drive, designed by Anton Skislewicz, 1939.

architectural training, and they probably considered themselves more builders than designers. Regardless, they were open to the aesthetic, cultural, and economic forces of the time, out of which they evolved an inviting style that was perfectly suited to its time and place.

Construction of Art Deco architecture on Miami Beach virtually ended with America's entrance into World War II. By 1941 most hotels had been taken over by the military to house soldiers in training, and almost all building materials were going to the war effort.

The upper part of Miami Beach remained a fancier destination, still reserved for monied Gentile clientele. NO DOGS OR JEWS ALLOWED signs were still posted in its hotels, while the lower beach resorts welcomed those who were forbidden access to the wealthier watering holes around the country and the world. These restrictions eased slightly after the stock market crash of 1929 destroyed the fortunes of much of the Beach's elite. But it was not until 1949 that GENTILES ONLY signs were banned from the Beach.

Like Jews, blacks were restricted from living on Miami Beach—and for decades longer. Even those who simply worked on the Beach were required to carry passes to get on and off the island. The singer Harry Belafonte broke the color barrier in 1963 by performing and staying at the Eden Roc. In 1964 the Civil Rights

The futuristic Plymouth Hotel at 336 21st Street, designed by Anton Skislewicz, 1940.

Act made discrimination on Miami Beach—and throughout the country—illegal.

As in most of white America, the 1950s returned the gloss of high times and carefree living to Miami Beach. Everything became bigger and bolder. The Fontainebleau Hotel, for example, opened on the former site of the Firestone estate on Millionaire's Row. A modern fantasy of French Provincial luxe, its architect, Morris Lapidus, established an altogether new style of resort glamor—flashy and formal, with sweeping curves, grand stairways (that could as likely as not lead to nowhere), and flamboyant illumination that included splashes of colored lighting.

Throughout most of the Fifties and Sixties, the area of the beach from First Street north to Lincoln Road and from the western, bay side of the island to the eastern, ocean side remained a mecca for retired, northern middle-class Jews, my grandmother among them. Countless weekends of my own childhood were spent driving across the MacArthur Causeway to visit her at one or another of the small Deco hotels where she lived season to season. Throughout her sixties and seventies, she walked to the ocean every day to swim. Her social life was conducted on the hotel verandas, where she was surrounded by legions of other Jewish grandmothers and grandfathers. While some referred to the Beach then as "God's Waiting

LEFT The Miami Beach Post Office at 1300 Washington Avenue, designed by Howard L. Cheney, 1939.
OVERLEAF The rhythmic geometry of a 1940s apartment complex.

Room," few places in the world actually offered as healthy, civilized, and amenable an environment to the Jewish elderly.

The 1970s were a bleak period for Miami Beach. Block after block of buildings fell into disrepair. A deadening monochromatic vogue of beige and brown washed over apartments, hotels, and retail stores alike, reducing all that remained of the island's original atmosphere of playfulness into a monotonous, indecipherable panorama. The once sparkling white facades with their painted pastel trims and rich, narrative ornamentation were buried alive under the drab palette and hodgepodge of signage that destroyed the unified facades.

Enter the *deus ex machina*: design writer Barbara Capitman, interior designer Leonard Horowitz, and a league of fledgling preservationists who saw the jewels in the faded Tropical Deco crown. Among that league were architectural photographers Steven Brooke and David Kaminsky; activists Richard Hoberman, Linda Polansky, Lynn Bernstein, Dennis Wilhelm, Michael Kinerk, and myself; graphic designer Woody Vondracek; design editor Gloria Blake; architect Bernard Zyscovich, and others. Our individual and collective visions for a restored and reenergized neighborhood grew into what is today the Miami Beach Art Deco District, also known as South Beach.

Barbara rose to the political battle.

A combination of faceted windows and rectangular "eyebrows" contributes to the exaggerated geometric richness of this architectural composition.

Leonard galvanized media attention with his radical new palette: whole facades in pink, pale green, light lemon, and powder blue. The world turned to look at Leonard's colors, and Barbara, poised for legislative action, secured the area's designation to the National Register of Historic Places. Ultimately, with preservation came renovation and with renovation, reinvention.

In 1981 I published *Tropical Deco, The Architecture and Design of Old Miami Beach,* and for the first time, the world got a comprehensive look, via David Kaminsky's photographs, at this forgotten and reevolving treasure. Steven Brooke's book, written by Barbara Capitman, was published in 1988, and the world was treated again to page after page of *Deco Delights.*

The first book on the revival of the international Art Deco style was published in London in 1968. Its cover was designed by Barry Zaid, a celebrated illustrator and longtime connoisseur of the style. Today Barry lives in one of the architectural gems of South Beach, a Venetian-style courtyard building built in the Twenties.

In the early 1980s, just as the preservation movement on the Beach was gaining a foothold, the Mariel boat lift from Cuba brought to Miami 125,000 refugees. Many settled in lower Miami Beach (known by then as the Art Deco district). By the mid-1980s, the neighborhood population consisted of a rapidly declining number of Jewish elderly and a

LEFT A 1950s pattern applied to an apartment façade.
OVERLEAF Architecture of the 1950s meets that of the 1920s on Ocean Drive.

burgeoning number of destitute Cuban refugees.

In 1984 the TV hit *Miami Vice* merged images of the neighborhood's seediness with its reemerging glamour, and again the nation took notice. Soon Deco buildings began to appear as backdrops for Calvin Klein's homoerotic underwear ads. Photographers, models, and agencies followed. Gays and artists moved in, and as in Key West, San Francisco, and TriBeCa, they renovated and decorated new life into the town. With the addition of cultural variety to its invaluable qualities of architectural harmony and pleasing scale, the Beach began to attract New Yorkers who flew in for weekends. Tourists arrived, nightclubs, galleries, and restaurants opened, and real estate developers flourished. Miami Beach was transfigured, and South Beach was officially born.

The momentum continued throughout the Nineties. The bright colors of the Caribbean began to appear on walls and furniture. Ocean Drive became a mecca for tourists and shoppers, and Lincoln Road, with a $16 million facelift, became one of the country's premiere restaurant rows. Stallone, Madonna, Michael Caine, and other stars opened clubs and yet more restaurants. Jewish bakeries metamorphosed into chic cafes, hardware stores and funeral parlors became clubs, and drugstores were transformed into boutiques. The island's legions of real estate buyers grew to include South Americans, Canadians, and Europeans. But with gentrification came the usual peril: the reinvention

LEFT Hotels built in the 1940s along the 1700 block of Collins Avenue.
OVERLEAF The Shelborne, 1801 Collins Avenue, designed by Igor Polivitsky, 1954.

that had saved the Beach began to threaten—and continues to threaten—its small-scale, pedestrian-friendly nature, indeed, its very soul.

Plans for a low-scale town built around Venetian-type canals at the southern end of the Beach were suddenly replaced with those for a mini-Manhattan. Giant glass condos rose high into the clouds at the beachfront. In 1998, however, a citizens' petition calling for a vote on stricter height control won Commission approval despite developers' multi-million dollar campaign against it. In 2001 Bernard Zyscovich conceived a master plan that would turn two blocks of surface parking on the north side of Lincoln Road into a Central Park–like gathering place.

South Beach has always been—and remains today—an urban neighbor-hood, one of the few remaining in this country. Its vitality and civility extend from its character, both urban and urbane. The preservation of this character is as essential as the preservation of its historic architecture. Vigilance and dedication to the full dimension of preservation is essential to perpetuate the quality of life in this unique, sun-soaked, and color-laden playground.

Laura Cerwinske

The name South Beach refers to the area of Miami Beach that extends from Government Cut on the South to Dade Boulevard on the north, and from the Atlantic Ocean on the east to Biscayne Bay on the west. Although a few of the locations shown in this book are located outside these literal boundaries, they are included because they faithfully express the spirit of South Beach.

Like its subtropical landscape, the South Beach color palette is extreme: cool blues and restful whites counteract heat and glare; Caribbean tones—flamingo pinks, peacock blues, and parrot greens— mirror the shameless vibrance of the panorama.

In pure and simple fact, South Beach exists because of its color. The allure of early Miami Beach derived from its low, white, pastel-trimmed buildings, the ever-blue ocean, and the wealth of breeze-blown, green palms. Add to this the molten beauty of "Greek light" that pours down across the landscape at "the blue hour," and you have one of the liveliest urban palettes in the world.

1

The
South Beach
Palette:
Color
and
Materials

COLOR

As recently as 1980 the South Beach palette was all but extinguished by the lurking doom of urban neglect and its concurrent "beige plague." Color, more than any other factor, proved the Beach's salvation. Lenny Horowitz, with his radical application of Necco Wafer colors, focused the fashion spotlight on the dying Art Deco district, and the world's eyes were opened.

From that time on, color has been the foremost tool of South Beach reinvention and marketing. Between Horowitz and *Miami Vice*, "Deco pink" became so overused during its era that it threatened to become the "beige of the Eighties." Ultimately, pinks, turquoises, and lavenders gave way to steamy, screaming Caribbean hues. The application of these darker tones in the Beach's bright climate proved almost as radical a gesture as Horowitz's earlier colors.

In the tropics and subtropics, natural tones are especially deep. The copper hues of the Caribbean and South America, as well as their purples and acid greens, diminish the intensity of glare and promote a greater sense of shade than pastels (which exist in nature only as accents, not as expanses).

Color—whether florid or subdued, vibrant or serene, hot or cool—remains foremost among South Beach's drawing powers. From Aegean white to caustic bright, the South Beach palette continues to evolve.

Details from the South Beach apartment of New York artist Ruth Marten.

MATERIALS

Climate, more than any other factor, dictates the materials appropriate to a region's interiors. South Beach's intense, humid summers and balmy winters call for hard, cool surfaces that resist dampness, heat, and mildew. In style, rooms must combine elegance with practicality, and glamour with durability. Since the region's very inception, glass block, tile, terrazzo, and stone have been consistently successful choices for application both inside and out.

GLASS BLOCK

A hallmark of modernity that originated with the German Bauhaus, glass block was commonly used in early Art Deco architecture. Its industrial refinement and block form emphasized that style's geometry. When first introduced during the 1930s, it was installed primarily in offices, stores, and factories. Soon, however, the light-filtering bricks were in demand for "up-to-date" houses: glass block conducts sunlight with little transmission of heat, allowing rooms to be permeated with cool translucence. It also offers effective sound insulation and requires no paint or polish.

A popular decorative choice in early Miami Beach, glass block, with its nautical look, enhanced the resort atmosphere of hotels, apartments, and winter homes. Later it was used in the form of room dividers for open-plan designs, offering a practical means

References to Parisian floral friezes, Aegean fluted columns, Babylonian ziggurats, and Hollywood geometry merge in a fireplace in an apartment once occupied by Art Deco District savior Barbara Capitman.

of defining spaces (such as living rooms, dining rooms, and kitchens) without separating them.

In the 1960s and Seventies, materials considered "modern" fell out of favor with architects and builders, and the demand for glass block ceased. One of its primary manufacturers, Pittsburgh Corning Glass, even announced the discontinuance of its production. But a number of designers, seeking the perpetuation of a classic twentieth-century building material, sucessfully petitioned for its revival.

Today glass block is available not only in its traditional variety of shapes and surfaces, but in colors and with rounded and hexagonal corners as well. It also comes in a variety of surfaces that includes flat and clear, wavy and translucent, prismlike and opaque—the last of which make excellent bathroom windows and shower stall walls.

KEYSTONE

Of all the materials inherent to the South Beach palette, keystone is likely the most elegant. An oolitic limestone, embedded with varieties of coral and exquisite fossils, it was originally quarried in the Florida Keys, hence its name. During the 1920s and Thirties, almost all the Mediterranean-style buildings and Art Deco hotels on the Beach used keystone as an element of their architectural or interior design. The original facade of the Bass Museum, built in 1930, was clad entirely in untinted keystone. Keystone door-surrounds, applied columns, and balustrades, many tinted in pink, cream, or seafoam green, appear in almost all the hotels along Ocean Drive. Quarried into extinction, the original keystone is no longer available. Excellent replicas, however, are made today.

RIGHT Cylindrical contours and geometric forms create an architectural sensuality in a modernist house. **OVERLEAF, ABOVE** Details of tinted coral rock, called keystone. **OVERLEAF, BELOW** An etched glass porthole window and a horizontal "wave" of glass block.

TERRAZZO

Cool and attractive, terrazzo has been used in South Beach since the 1920s, when it was installed in many of Miami Beach's winter estates. It became a popular choice for the early Deco hotels not only because it was climatically appropriate, but also because it offered a means of introducing decoration into resort interiors at little expense. Tinted cement embedded with marble chips, terrazzo floors could be composed in colors of almost any combination and patterns of almost any density and shape. The most common design motifs to appear in the floors of Tropical Deco buildings were waves, stripes, geometric patterns, and hotel logos.

The earliest terrazzo floors in South Beach were composed of deep pinks or corals, yellows and shades of seafoam green. The 1940s brought an even lighter range of hues, which gave way to a rage for earth tones in the 1950s. During the 1960s and Seventies, terrazzo, like glass block, fell out of favor. The universality of air-conditioning in South Beach interiors obscured climate consciousness, and wall-to-wall carpeting and the dreaded shag rug nearly obliterated its use.

Terrazzo has resurged in popularity over the last decade. With the restoration of countless South Beach buildings, pristine terrazzo floors have emerged from under layers of carpet and linoleum. Their untarnished gloss and appealing colors and patterns continue to inspire both imitation and reinterpretation.

PRECEDING PAGES, LEFT Wall panels of opaque glass called Vitrolite. **PRECEDING PAGES, RIGHT** Exquisitely sculpted cast-metal panels in the bathroom of the Wolfsonian. **LEFT** Terrazzo floor patterns from the lobby of the elegant Tides hotel on Ocean Drive.

TILE

Tile, unlike glass block, possesses a lineage that extends as far back as ancient history. Today tiles continue to be celebrated as "a means of decoration which for beauty of effect, durability, and inexpensive cost has scarcely a parallel." While many of today's most popular tiles are imported from Mexico, Spain, Italy, and France, many local manufacturers handcraft tiles in the same tradition as their European forebears.

In South Beach, the variety of tiles ranges from densely patterned antique Spanish examples to pristine monochromatic contemporary squares. The exuberant mosaics that were popularly applied to floors in the 1920s and Thirties can still be found today in the courtyards of many Mediterranean-style buildings. Equally dramatic yet more contemporary are the bold, colorful tile treatments given to the floors and walls of many newer homes, stores, and restaurants. Glazed tiles are well suited for application to interior walls and counters as well as garden walls and even garden "floors."

RIGHT AND OVERLEAF The richness of Spain's Alhambra is replicated on stairways and floors.
PAGES 74–75 A "tile carpet" in the garden of the Delano hotel.

THE FROZEN FOUNTAIN

The Frozen Fountain, like stylized flower motifs, was among the most popular of the original French Art Deco designs. Its surging symmetry and curvaceous fluidity heightened the style's geometric drama. At the great 1925 Paris *Exposition des Arts Décoratifs* it was referred as *le jet d'eau* by the famed Art Deco glass artist René Lalique.

This patterned cascade expresses the rising and falling of water—the welling up of a natural force and its descent—thereby symbolizing life. For Floridians it also aptly makes an allusion to Ponce de Leon's Fountain of Youth.

H istorically, fantasy architecture has been an indulgence limited to the aristocracy. Until American popular culture inundated the far reaches of the globe, only pharaohs, conquerers, kings, and queens could delight in seeing their imaginary worlds spring fully realized to life. Think Marie Antoinette and her Laiterie, Catherine the Great and her peasant's hut–style country retreat, and, of course, the eternal domiciles of the pharaohs.

This royal precedent of theme architecture was drawn into modern tradition by resort designers whose creations took the form of everything from rustic Adirondack camps in the Gothic style to motel courts shaped like wigwams, from buildings in the design of pyramids to interiors reminiscent of Busby Berkeley backdrops. The greatest showman of this tradition, Morris Lapidus, coined his style "the architecture of joy." Lapidus is best known for the interiors he designed in the Fifties for the Fontainebleau and Eden Roc hotels. With walls of light, undulating lines, and reinvented classical forms, he provided an unintimidating experience of grandeur. Unbound by modernist notions of purity, the heirs to Lapidus today create formal environments that are equally eclectic and playful.

2

Hotels
Restaurants
Clubs
Cinemas
Museums

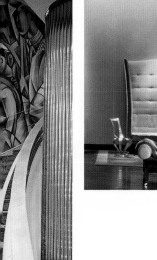

HOTELS

DELANO

Built in 1947, the winged-topped Delano has always stood as a centerpiece of the South Beach skyline. In 1995 famed hotelier Ian Schrager hired French haute designer Philippe Starck to have his way with the resort's "grande dame," and in so doing, revived the lost art of "swank."

Delano is at once sumptuous and casual, sensual and stark, glowing and reclusive. Its design evoked the lost art of "lobby socializing," making every corner and seating arrangement as much a comfortable gathering place as a photo opportunity awaiting its moment. A feeling of being simultaneously indoors and outdoors extends from the monumental entry terrace, through the lobby, and out onto the grand rear terrace that overlooks the pool, gardens, and seaside village. Throughout the interiors and the landscaped gardens, oversized and mismatched furnishings add an Alice-in-Wonderland sense of fantasy.

PRECEDING PAGES Various seating groupings in the dramatic hotel lobby. **RIGHT AND OVERLEAF**
The breakfast buffet and "breakfast table." **PAGE 88** South Beach style items in the gift shop.
84
PAGE 89 Delano bar. **PAGES 90–91** The hotel's terraced rear garden.

THE TIDES

When The Tides first opened in
1936, it was, at ten floors, the tallest
hotel on Miami Beach. Designed by
the noted architect L. Murray Dixon,
it remains today the tallest original
Art Deco structure on the island.
During World War II, like many other
oceanfront hotels, The Tides was
used as a barracks for American
military troops.

In 1997, The Tides, renovated by

Island Outpost, opened once again as a luxury hotel, its 115 original rooms converted into 45 spacious rooms and suites. A AAA Four-Diamond restaurant, called 1220, and a bar were added adjacent to the restored lobby. Alfresco dining on The Terrace, the ocean-facing front veranda, allows guests an uninterrupted view of street theater along Ocean Drive.

SMALL HOTELS AND GUEST HOUSES

Like any true city, South Beach offers accommodations both grand and intimate. Its wealth of smaller hotels, most built during the 1930s, are known for their casual ease. Many of them, nevertheless, provide the amenities common to larger hotels—their own restaurants, pools, and private sitting rooms.

THE HOTEL

Originally known as the Tiffany Hotel, this South Beach landmark was built in 1939 by premier Miami Beach architect L. Murray Dixon. In the late 1990s urban pioneer Tony Goldman, who has refurbished and reinvented more than eighteen local properties, joined creative forces with fashion designer Todd Oldham. The result was the application of a 1950s–60s palette—and a totally new look—for this classic example of Art Deco architecture. The Hotel has a rooftop pool and courtyard dining.

PRECEDING PAGES Original porthole windows dramatize the lobby of The Hotel.
LEFT AND ABOVE The bar and dining room. Left photograph by Carlos Domenech

HOTEL ASTOR

The Hotel Astor, built in 1936, has forty rooms, a full-service concierge, and a private pool.

ABOVE The lantern hangs above the Hotel Astor dining room.
RIGHT The lobby of the hotel, with its original terrazzo floors.

THE IMPALA

The Impala, also built in the 1930s, is a
seventeen-room boutique hotel
entered, like an oasis, through a garden
courtyard. Rooms are provided with
European linens and down pillows and
their walls colored in soft, restful tones. It
also has its own Italian restaurant, Spiga.

ABOVE A sitting room, tailored and commodious, in this hideaway in the heart of South Beach.

104 All floors throughout are paved in Saturnia stone. **RIGHT** The sleek, updated bathroom.

THE MERMAID GUEST HOUSE

In addition to small hotels, there are even smaller guest houses. These offer their own individual styles of informality, personality, and charm, ideal for youthful and more economical travelers.

The Mermaid was originally a ten-room apartment building. Owners Ana and Gonzalo Torres converted it into a colorful, romantic guest house, Caribbean in its appeal to their artist and musician friends.

MIRADOR

Mirador is a 1,200-unit, amenities-filled rental apartment complex overlooking Biscayne Bay. Built in the mid-1960s, it was renovated and conceptually reinvigorated by the architecture firm of Zyscovich, Inc., as the quintessence of South Beach–style living. Its leasing office is a subtle and highly polished allusion to that sensual and recreational appeal.

PRECEDING PAGES Furnishings were selected to make the leasing office feel more like the home the potential renter could have than like a business venue. **LEFT** The conference room is available to renters for private use. **ABOVE** A view to the cabana-style offices from the conference room. Soft white cotton cabana curtains gently move with the breeze of carefully directed air currents. All photographs by Patricia Fisher.

111

The leasing office's six elegant "cabanas" (conference rooms) surround a sparkling, relaxed "living room" (reception area) whose height and bright white walls extend the light-filled ambience.

A model studio apartment.
Photograph by Patricia Fisher.

Mirador health bar and gym.

RESTAURANTS

TAP-TAP

In Haiti, minibuses, a prime form of transportation, are mobile art works, brilliantly decorated and colorful. They are called tap-taps. In 1993 the American philanthropist and documentary filmmaker Katharine Kean, out of her appreciation for the Haitian people and their culture, decided to open a

Haitian restaurant on South Beach. She filled its five rooms with murals, tabletop paintings, and artifacts by Haitian artists and called the restaurant Tap-Tap.

Tap-Tap serves a traditional Haitian menu: griyo (fried pork), conch creole, akra (malanga fritters). The food and its presentation are as colorful as the restaurant. A visit to Tap-Tap is like a quick trip to the Caribbean—without leaving South Beach's shores.

PRECEDING PAGES, RIGHT *The Speculator* by Daleus. **LEFT** *The Kids* by Briere.

Ezile Freda, the light-skinned Madonna, by Jude Papaloko.

RIGHT *Rara* by Jude Papaloko. **OVERLEAF** *The Wedding*, a

table painting by Daleus. **PAGES 126–27** The Briere room.

TANTRA

The ancient Indian tantric arts evolved to heighten the senses as a means of elevating consciousness. Locate a nexus of tantric intention in the context of South Beach hedonism, and you have Tantra, the restaurant/lounge. Owner Tim Hogle designed the interior as a sensory immersion—the floor is a lawn of grass, the lighting dreamlike, and the art evocative.

All the statuary in Tantra is imported from India. Paintings are by South American and Miami artists.

CLUBS

PEARL AND NIKKI BEACH CLUB

When restaurateurs Jack and Lucia Penrod teamed with night club impressarios Tommy "Pooch" Puccio and Eric Omores, their intention was to create "six acres of paradise." Out of their dream came Pearl, a restaurant and champagne lounge that overlooks a sandy playground called Nikki Beach.

Pooch proudly refers to the result as "the eighth wonder of the world."

A visit to Pearl is like entering the inside of a conch shell—all dreamy iridescence and glow. "Here everyone seems ten years younger," says Pooch. Outside, the fantasy continues: designer Stephane Dupous provided tepees for changing, lounging, and other South Beach nightlife recreation.

CINEMAS

LINCOLN CENTER

As a former chairman of the Miami Design Preservation League, architect Bernard Zyscovich is known throughout South Florida as a keen preservationist. Thus, his choice as designer of "the new gateway" to Lincoln Road—the Regal Cinemas—was hardly surprising. His decision, however, "to build something totally modern" was, indeed.

The eighteen-theater cinema, now known as "Lincoln Center," is both bold and brilliant. Colorful, animated, and highly faceted, it fits perfectly into the traditional South Beach style, while its sweeping modernism and irregular angles suit the South Beach spirit. Zyscovich harkened to the great movie palaces of the early twentieth century for inspiration, designing "a grand entrance, a fabulous lobby, and an outrageous architectural statement." At the same time, he reached for a distinct twenty-first-century expression, giving the project a quality of "techno-drama."

PRECEDING PAGES AND RIGHT A geometric pattern of colored glass panels wraps the entire façade. Backlit at night, it becomes a veil of color through which Lincoln Road pedestrians can observe the activity within. Escalators appear to soar, suspended in space. The second floor in the two-story-high lobby is reached by a monumental staircase.

MUSEUMS

THE WOLFSONIAN

Heir to a Miami movie theater fortune, the collector Mitchell Wolfson, Jr. amassed a vast assemblage of Decorative and Propaganda Arts—furniture, paintings, books, prints, industrial and decorative art objects, and ephemera from the late nineteenth to the mid-twentieth centuries. The Wolfsonian was founded in

LIVERPOOL JOHN MOORES UNIVERSITY
LEARNING SERVICES

1986 to exhibit, document, and preserve this collection. In 1997 it became a division of Florida International University (FIU) when Wolfson donated his collection and museum facility to the university. This was the largest gift ever contributed to a public university in Florida. The museum explores through its exhibitions and special programs the role of design at the height of the industrial age in social, political, and technological contexts.

The Wolfsonian is housed in a 1927 Mediterranean Revival building, which in 1992 was renovated and enlarged as a seven-story, 56,000-square-foot, state-of-the-art facility. Miami architect Mark Hampton designed the renovation in association with architect Billy Kearns.

In addition to exhibition galleries, the museum includes an auditorium and gift/book shop, administrative offices, and library. The Wolfsonian's conservation lab and remaining object collections are housed in The Annex, a 28,000-square-foot historic warehouse, also located in South Beach.

PAGES148–49 The restored terra-cotta façade decoration from the Norris Theater of Norristown, Pennsylvania, is the centerpiece of the main entrance atrium of The Wolfsonian Foundation. Manufactured by Conkling Armstrong in 1929, the façade was originally installed over the entrance and marquee of the Norris Theater. It was rescued along with two three-panel art-glass windows when the theater was demolished in 1983. **PRECEDING PAGES** Originally Washington Storage, this 1927 Mediterranean Revival building, designed by Robertson and Patterson, housed the personal and household items of winter residents when they returned north. The Wolfsonian is located at 1001 Washington Avenue. **RIGHT** A detail of the lobby's handpainted ceilng. **OVERLEAF** The library reading room.

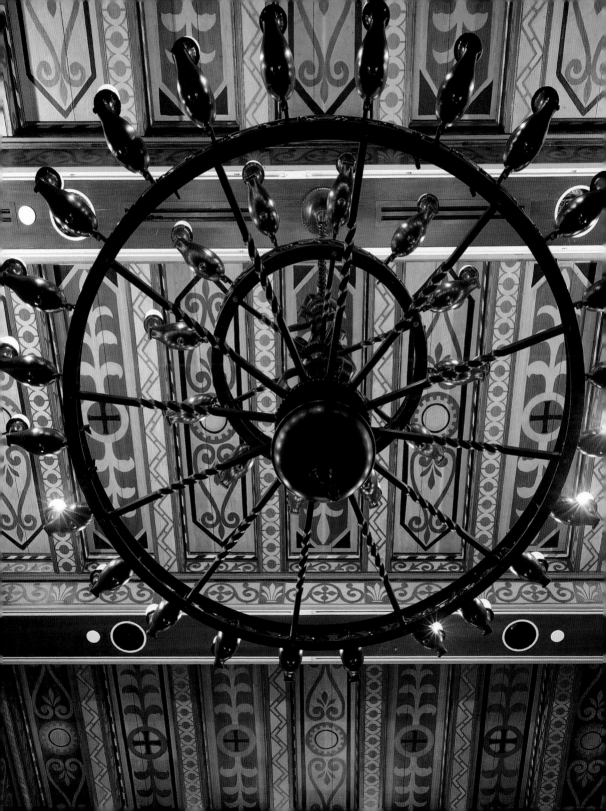

PRECEDING PAGES The conference room. **RIGHT** In the previous Wolfsonian offices are *Neon Flamingos*, designed for Mitchell Wolfson, Jr. **OVERLEAF, LEFT** Iron gate, 1925, designed by A. Mazzucotelli. **OVERLEAF, RIGHT** On the table is a model of the Theme Center for the 1939 New York World's Fair, designed in 1937 by Wallace K. Harrison and J. André Fouilhoux, architects. At right is an Italian papier-mâché lamp.

BASS MUSEUM

Pioneer Miami architect Russell Pancoast designed the original Art Deco museum building in 1930. More than half a century later, Arata Isozaki, a major innovator and thinker in world architecture, created a 25,000-foot expansion. Together they provide a confluence of civic and artistic functions that makes the museum an urban cornerstone of Miami Beach:

the original building now houses a lecture hall/gallery, cafe, and offices, while the addition serves as an exhibition hall.

Founded with a donation of some 500 works of art from the private collection of Miami Beach residents John and Johanna Bass, the museum now maintains a collection of some 3,000 works. These encompass European fine arts and decorative arts from the fifteenth century to the present; North American, Latin American, Caribbean and Asian art from the seventh century to the present; textiles, tapestries and ecclesiastical vestments and artifacts; photographs; modern and contemporary design objects; and architectural photographs and drawings that document the design history of Miami Beach. The Isozaki addition serves as a showcase for temporary exhibitions, primarily of contemporary art.

PRECEDING PAGES The Bass Museum at 2121 Park Avenue. The geometric classicism of the original, keystone-clad museum building was inspired by Mayan architecture and includes carved stone bas-reliefs designed by Gustav Bohland over the entrance. **LEFT** The addition by Arata Isozaki consists of two rectangular volumes posed at an angle to each other. Photograph by Peter Harholdt

166 The museum addition and reflecting pool by
Arata Isozaki. Photograph by Peter Harholdt.

DACRA DEVELOPMENT

Craig Robins is founder, president, and owner of DACRA Development, one of South Beach's most prominent real estate development companies. From the late 1980s to the late Nineties, a time of dynamic artistic activity on the island, he lived in the Webster Hotel on Ocean Drive. His 2,500-square-foot apartment on two floors served both as home and gallery.

Robins's art-collecting passion, begun in college, demanded suitable space and place for connoisseurship. The experience of living with a collection taught him how to incorporate art into his way of life. Thus, when he opened his company office, art was as much a feature as his commercial dreams.

Robins's art collection fills not only his South Beach DACRA office, but the new home he shares with his wife, Ivelyn, and an office in the Miami Design District. The work is international and includes artists from diverse ethnic backgrounds. Robins attended the University of Barcelona in 1972, and his early tastes showed the influence of Picasso, Dalí, and Miró. Today his collection continues to express a Spanish emphasis with distinctly modernist inclinations. "I am attracted to that which has impact on our time," says Robins. "As with my life, the collection is constantly evolving."

PRECEDING PAGES The centerpiece of the conference room is *Con Licencia* by Jose Bedia, 1990. **RIGHT** *Clement Greenberg* by John Baldessari, 1966–68. **OVERLEAF** *Names (1001 Utilidades)* by Jac Leirner, 1989.

GREENBERG

...GMENTS ARE GIVEN AND CONTAINED
...TE EXPERIENCE OF ART.
...E WITH IT; THEY ARE NOT ARRIVED AT
...HROUGH REFLECTION OR THOUGHT.
...GMENTS ARE ALSO INVOLUNTARY;
...O MORE CHOOSE WHETHER OR NOT
...RK OF ART THAN YOU CAN CHOOSE
...R TASTE SWEET OR LEMONS SOUR.
...R NOT ESTHETIC JUDGMENTS ARE
...PORTED IS ANOTHER MATTER.)

PRECEDING PAGES *People on Fire* by Guillermo Kuitca, 1993. **LEFT** *Who Am I* and *House with Bamboo Trees and Court Lady* by Anne Chu, both 1999. **OVERLEAF, LEFT** *In Spirit* by Carlos Alfonzo, 1987. **OVERLEAF, RIGHT** *Untitled* by Enrique Castro-Cid, 1972.

PAGES 182–83 *Loudness is a Force (or the Modern Prometheus)* by Thaddeus Strode, 1990. **PAGES 184–85** *Oranges*, two paintings by Roberto Juarez, 1995, frame a work at center by Ruben Torres-Llorca. **PRECEDING PAGES** *In Flesh* by Carlos Alfonzo, 1987. **LEFT** *Head #5* by C. Alfonzo and *Untitled* by Robert Llimos, 1998.

DECORATIVE DETAILS

Decorative details are the grace notes of architectural design. South Beach is a treasury of colorful, narrative, fanciful, and graphic details. These embellishments are most abundant in the historic district, where they appear as architectural ornaments, sculptural reliefs, and tile and terrazzo patterns. Classical motifs and geometric designs are among the most popular.

Photographs by Barry Zaid

191

Few other places in the world
provide such hospitality to
unique art collections as South
Beach. Its natural appeal to
collectors of "serious" art is as
strong as its appeal to "serious
collectors of the ridiculous." But
then, consider the city's original
art form—the souvenir.

The homes in this chapter
celebrate not only the character
of their collections, but also the
power of recollection—of an era,
a place, an atmosphere—each as
enchanting as it is ephemeral.

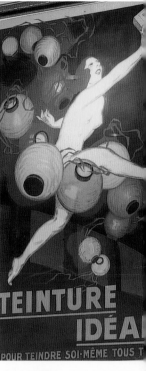

3

Homes:
Collections
and
Recollections

ANTONI HOUSE

Brian Antoni, author of the South Beach–set novels *Paradise Overdose* and *Naked Came the Manatee,* is a connoisseur of the wierd, the overlooked, and the discarded. His 1920s-era South Beach house is a temple to Florida high camp, a room-by-room testament to its owner's skill in discovering treasure, even in streetside discards.

PRECEDING PAGES In the corner of the dining room is a 1920s ironwork lighting feature. The chandeliers were found in thrift stores. **LEFT** The theme of the bedroom came from sunflowers growing outside. **ABOVE** The Wall of Terrible Portraits, of which not one cost more than ten dollars. **OVERLEAF** Antoni found the alligator wrestling sign blown onto the Tamiami Trail after Hurricane Andrew.

Nearly buried behind an imposing tangle of shrubs and debris, the derelict house had been inhabited for more than sixty years by a recluse. Many years later, Antoni is still clearing it out.

Ultimately the house provided the ideal setting for Antoni's various collections of bad art and high kitsch, all of which he's found traversing the state of Florida between Key West and Okeechobee. Characteristically, the collections are tropically nostalgic, weird, and/or humorous, and each borders on the surreal. Every piece "has to make a statement, everything has to imply something," he explains.

Museums occasionally borrow Antoni's "art" for exhibition. "I've become an 'official lender' of stuff I picked up off the ground," he laughs.

Antoni's South Beach residential style is in marked contrast to that of his classically modernist apartment in Manhattan, where he lives part time. "In an environment this ridiculous, how can you worry?" The very purchase of the house portended this philosophy: he snapped it off the market, on a Friday, before he was even insured, thinking, "What are the chances of a hurricane happening over the weekend?" That Sunday Hurricane Andrew hit. Ridiculous.

LEFT In the porch, the mermaid fin is made of goldleafed Baskin-Robbins tasting spoons. The table top is the state of Florida. The alligator came from a circus. **RIGHT** The door surround is original keystone.

SANDERSON-BRADY HOUSE

Lee Brady and David Sanderson's Bauhaus-style residence was the first International Style or "modern" house built on Miami Beach. It was designed in 1946 by Anton Polivitsky, who called for a construction of solid, poured concrete and provided for sweeping interior spaces, flowing Noguchi-like soffits, and expansive views to the gardens.

So distinctive was the design that *Life* magazine named it the "House of the Future." Capitalizing on its drama, Cadillac parked a car inside the living room and photographed an ad there.

After a long and colorful epoch as party boy entrepreneurs, Sanderson and Brady moved to Miami Beach. Today, Brady, working under the name Mythos, creates sculptures as visionary representatives of his own personal mythology. He shapes haunting images of dogs' faces out of palm husks and grass fibers and then unites and decorates them with copper, iron, 23-karat gold and sterling silver leaf, Tibetan turquoise, amethyst, and topaz. The fragility of the natural materials, combined with the metaphysical properties of the various stones and metals, enhances the sculptures' paradoxical quality. Brady's intent is to "create magical beings as talismans of an imagined world of harmony and unconditional love."

PRECEDING PAGES In the living room, *Astrocharger* by Brazier-Jones sits on the table in front of the 1920s sofa. Above the mantel is a lithograph by d'Ylen, 1930, flanked by works by self-taught artist George Colin. At far left is *4 AM* by Lee Brady. On the mantel is the bronze *Herma*, 1975, by Man Ray, his last sculpture; an Art Deco bronze and ivory archer by Uriano, 1931; and a gilded Thai bronze, 1840. The two columns flanking the mantel are from Crete, A.D. 100. **RIGHT** A corner of the living room. The signed Corbusier chaise, at right, is one of the first thousand produced. The Chinese gong is nineteenth-century bronze with a teak and brass stand.

Lee Brady's dog-mask sculptures, standing on and around a gilded Tibetan prayer table, comprise a "Mythos" altar. A Japanese wedding kimono is draped below it. The slender late nineteenth-century African wood sculpture is from the Cenufi tribe of the Ivory Coast. Above it is a Brazilian painting of tribal dancers. **207**

KNAPP
HOUSE

Is it a sculpture or is it a toy? Is it a
religious artifact or a kitsch
souvenir? Was it made by an artist
or a child, by an insane person or
an enlightened one? Artist Dina
and poet Jeffrey Knapp invoke the
spirit of the naive by filling their
house with Haitian art and the
work of self-taught artists.

The cartoonish faces of Satans, saints, and sequined Madonnas peer out from every wall or surface not filled with books. What difference who made these objects or what their intention? Each playful work is uniquely transporting.

The couple began amassing art in the mid-1970s when Jeffrey Knapp, then a poet in residence in Key West, first discovered Haitian art. Both he and Dina were drawn by the works' naïveté and strong religious spirit. "As religious individuals and visual artists, we respond to religious cultures that incorporate visual objects," they explain. "From the moment we first saw this work, we had to live with it."

Years later, on trips to North Georgia, where they drove their daughter to summer camp, the Knapps came across the work of American self-taught artists (formerly known as "outsider" artists).

PRECEDING PAGES In the Knapp living room are, at the left of the sofa, *Baby Angel* by Howard Finster and a black cat in cut and painted wood by Tubby Brown. In front of the window is a cut-tin devil by R. A. Miller. To its right is a mud painting by Jimmy Lee Suddath. **LEFT** Paintings by Purvis Young hang over the mantel and stand at the left of the fireplace.

211

They found the expressiveness of this work strongly akin to that of Haitian art, and their annual summer trips became a means of visiting the region's artists. Back at home, they discovered the work of the Miami artist Purvis Young, whose naive-looking paintings and drawings have gained consistent recognition over the last decade. In 1999 Young's entire studio was purchased by internationally known art collectors Don and Mera Rubell, whose family owns South Beach's Albion Hotel.

Their "amassing" experience led Jeffrey Knapp to coauthor the book *Self-Taught Florida Artists.* "Amassing is different from— more than—collecting," they explain. "It represents the complete weaving of all aspects of our lives."

PRECEDING PAGES The Knapp bedroom hosts the patterns, textiles, and colors of the 1950s. **LEFT** The bedroom of daughter Ariel, with a Haitian sequined bottle on the windowsill and a *lea* or Haitian banner on the wall at left. Photograph by Matthew Fuller.

KARLOCK
HOUSE

Kent Karlock loves flea market
shopping. Before moving to Miami,
he amassed a collection of antique
European furniture and art from the
flea markets of New York, Florence,
Paris, and London. Once at home in
South Beach, he concentrated on
"what was most available—pieces
from the Seventies."

While lacking the finesse and intricacy of the antique, the sleek sofas, chrome lamps, and glass tabletops of the late modern era fit comfortably into the South Beach setting. The cool, reflective surfaces welcome the abundant sunlight that fills the house and draw the garden setting inside. "The move required a definite change of taste," he explains, "but I'm liking this style more and more. It's easy, casual, and because of the specific materials, there's no worry about insects, humidity, or heat. I don't have to be concerned about the climate's effects on textiles, wood, leather, or paint—things that mildew, flake, or peel."

Karlock's house, built in 1953, was originally a warren of small rooms. What appealed to him most was the possibilty of creating a twenty-eight-foot-square great room, an expanse he could fill with the fruits of his collecting passion. To create the uninterrupted space, he tore out the existing living room, two bedrooms, a bathroom, and a closet and installed French doors that open onto the pool and patio. This great room, dense with furniture, books, and art, manages to feel sweeping and enveloping at once, an effect that—like Karlock's earlier taste, is quite European.

PRECEDING PAGES The high kitsch, late-1930s mural that stretches across the living room wall was originally painted for an ocean liner by an artist who signed the work "Wilcke." In the foreground is a collection of French and Belgian art pottery. **RIGHT** The Tulip chair is by Eero Saarinen. In the foreground is a classic Marcel Breuer chair. **OVERLEAF, LEFT** The leather settee at rear is by the American designer Harvey Probber. **OVERLEAF, RIGHT** An eclectic collection of modernist and classical decorative arts.

ZAID
APARTMENT

Ten years ago, illustrator/
designer Barry Zaid, then
living in Manhattan's Upper
West Side, saw an ad for an
apartment for sale in a
picturesque Italianate
building in the center of
South Beach. He flew down
the next day, purchased it,

and turned it into his Miami design studio. Six years later, when an identical apartment on the floor above became available, he took it over for his living space. The commute is thirteen steps.

Downstairs is all business. Well, almost. In one room, an Italian Beidermeier conference table looks out onto a verdant tropical garden. A stack of prototype cat houses in various architectural styles flanks white painted French doors. An entire wall is lined with shelves of art reference books culled from years of illustrating for publications including the *London Times*, English *Vogue*, the *New York Times*, *New York* magazine, and numerous books for children and adults. One, *Wish You Were Here*, published in 1990, featured numerous old postcards of Miami Beach hotels. "I never imagined that within two years I would actually be living here," he muses.

His bedroom upstairs looks like a monk's cell in a palazzo, furnished only with a futon on the floor, but with crown molding (which he added) and deep baseboards. Walls of the palest yellow are enlivened by shiny white woodwork. The floor itself is Florida native pine, stained a Tiffany robin's egg blue. The room, which has five windows, seems to float on light. Pictures, mostly his own or those of artist friends, sit informally on the floor, allowing them to be moved around at will. An Ionic capital on wheels, a plaster elephant pedestal, and a stuffed cotton tabby are among the ever-changing group of toys and decorative items.

PRECEDING PAGES The cartoonlike butler stands were designed and made by Zaid. The throne chair is a replica of a throne now in the Cairo Museum. The original, from a tomb discovered in 1905, belonged to Sitamun, a cousin of Tutankamun. **OVERLEAF** A painting by Zaid sits beside his futon bed. **PAGES 228–29** Ironstone pitchers and prettily painted Poole pottery were found in London's Portobello market. Gaudy mugs and elephant candlesticks come from New York's Chinatown. A blue-and-white Charles and Diana Royal Wedding teapot and brown-and-white plates were found at garage sales. A box of Celestial Seasonings tea, which Zaid designed, sits on a shelf over the stove.

The dining area, looking out into a giant banyan tree, has only a Victorian cast-iron restaurant table and two knockoff Arne Jacobsen molded plywood "ant" chairs. The third chair, a replica of a throne now in the Cairo Museum, belongs to Zaid's beloved seventeen-year-old cat, Earl Grey. A pair of lacy whitewashed Indian screens placed against a periwinkle blue wall admits a mosaic of light while providing privacy. The 1950s faux-chinois chandelier, already an item of kitsch, has been irreverently decorated with Christmas bubblelights and a mini disco ball, echoing a pair of decoupaged Victorian glass globes that rest on bracketed English majolica sconces. Mitzi the Maid, Reg the Butler, and Cowboy Tex are samples from a line of animated hand-painted side tables Zaid designed during his years in Colorado.

RIGHT A rusted medicine chest was replaced with a white-framed mirror and shelf that holds a collection of antique tins and one of the Florence Gunnarson bath oil boxes Zaid designed. **OVERLEAF** The garden Zaid created, which fills the view from his windows.

WILHELM-KINERK
HOUSE

Michael Wilhelm and Dennis
Kinerk, authors of *Rediscovering Art
Deco USA* and *Popcorn Palaces*, are
among the founders of the Miami
Design Preservation League. They
are also among South Beach's most
passionate collectors of Art Deco
furniture and decorative arts.
Accordingly, their house—built in

PRECEDING PAGES Inside the cabinet is a collection of Fiestaware. The Humpty-Dumpty cookie jar on top is Brush McCoy from the 1930s. The clock is a 1950s Telechron. **LEFT** The brass female figure atop the 1930s Philco radio is circa 1930s. The poster is from the 1934 Chicago World's Fair. **ABOVE** The handles of the fireplace tools and andirons are Steuben crystal. The fireplace is faux finish wood with black lacquer and backlit glass block.

1933—is a showplace of period design. What's more, it is expansive enough to accommodate their two pianos (one, a baby grand), a burled Carpathian elm dining table, sideboard, and serving cart (designed by the noted Eldon F. Baldauf), and their Art Deco bedroom suite with fourteen-foot-long headboard.

A massive collection of vivid Fiestaware mirrors the colors of original Vitrolite wall panels, tinted mirrors, and period glass and ceramic collectibles. Bronze nymphets gesture with sinewy lyricism from various settings. Glass and ceramic objects echo both the colors and style of their surroundings.

Wilhelm and Kinerk looked at over seventy houses before purchasing this one. With its keystone columns with dolphin-motif capitals, sunken tub on a Vitrolite dais, and fireplace with classic nautical-design frieze, the correctness of their choice is indisputable.

LEFT A Nuart ash receiver is from the late 1930s.
RIGHT An alabaster lamp with silk shade and a Frankart potmetal silhouette lamp, circa 1930.

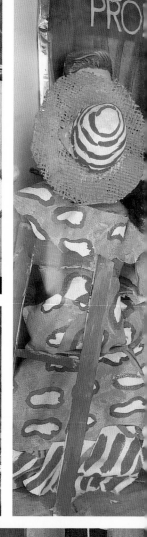

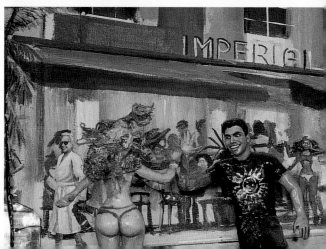

THE
SCULL SISTERS

They are as colorful as Fiestaware, as sweet as guava pasteles, and as animated as a Disney cartoon. In fact, not only do they claim Walt Disney as one of their great inspirations (along with Goya and Toulouse-Lautrec), but they also share his birthday. Haydee and Sahara Scull—Cuban-born identical twin artists—have made jubilant depictions of the South Beach street life their signature image. Their three-dimensional canvases and murals derive from the tradition of painterly folk art. Naive, pictorial, and highly narrative, they express a robust innocence, a romantic celebration of the urban seaside settings in which they live.

Working from a combination of photographs, real life, and memory, the Scull Sisters produce private commissions, portaits, and murals. Haydee paints in the scenic backgrounds to which Sahara adds detailing. Then Haydee sculpts in clay paste the dimensional figures that populate the paintings—often images of themselves. Haydee's son Miguel, who works with the sisters full time, designs the artworks' architectural effects and other special details.

South Beach's substantial population of New Yorkers, Europeans, and South Americans accounts significantly for its cosmopolitan flavor. These residents, whether weekend regulars, annual visitors, or permanent transplants, bring to the design and decoration of their South Beach homes a distinct worldliness.

4

Homes:
Exotic and
Exuberant

LEDDICK
HOUSE

David Leddick's two-story carriage
house is unmistakably of another
era. It was constructed with garages
and an apartment for servants
downstairs, and, upstairs, a beautiful
floor that the owners planned to
live in only while their main house
was being built on the grounds.
After the 1929 stock market crash,

however, the owners lost their fortune and the larger residence was never built.

Leddick is the beneficiary of the original owners' superior tastes. The floors are covered in marble with ornamental tile details. Venetian-style columns divide the public rooms, and a ceiling of native pecky cypress lends not only rustic elegance, but natural heat and termite resistance. In fact, between the beautiful high ceilings and the marble floors, the house stays cool enough that Leddick uses no air-conditioning. Even more unusual, the house was in such good condition when the author purchased it in 1997 that he had to undertake very little renovation. This made it the perfect accommodation for a man who, after four careers—naval officer, dancer, advertising/creative director, televison commercial director—savors the tranquillity of his writing desk.

PRECEDING PAGES The entry was designed so that cars could drive right through the carriage house. The 1940s ornamental plaques above the door were salvaged from a pink 1950s dining room. Leddick's writing desk is a large 1930s dining table. The Venetian ivory bust is from the 1920s. The red lacquered box with Caribbean slave beads on top is from India. In the front hall, at left, is an eighteenth-century English gaming table. **ABOVE** The bathroom with its original pecky cypress paneling. **RIGHT** In the study, a sixteenth-century Portugese table from Macao holds Leddick's collection of nineteenth- and twentieth-century bronze, porcelain, wood, and cast-cement sculptures. The mirror, at right, is eighteenth-century Italian.

ABOVE The 1920s French bedroom suite is from the early floral Art Deco period. Originally it was given by the French government to an American aviatrix who was in France with a group of women fliers headed by Amelia Earhart. The woman returned to Miami Beach, married, and kept the furniture for the rest of her life. Leddick found it in a local antique store. The photograph on the dresser is by George Platt Lynes. The French ceramic bust of Joan of Arc is from the 1920s, a period in which she was venerated. The drawing to the right is by Pavel Tchelitchev. **RIGHT** The lion's head, a symbol of Venice, appears on the knocker of the Venetian-style door.

LANZA
HOUSE

Bianca Lanza had lived in three
South Beach locations before
moving to her present home on
a street unique for its quiet and
privacy. Designed in the 1930s by
L. Murray Dixon, the house was
built originally as a single family
residence. Later owners turned it

into an eight-unit complex, then a five-unit compound.

When she first purchased the property in 1996, the house was in poor condition and an uncomfortably small accommodation for Lanza and her teenage son. Her approach to renovation was tidy but complex: combine the cramped kitchen with a tiny existing bath and make one good-sized kitchen; add an arch where the house orginally ended and enclose the outdoor patio to create an indoor living room; conscript one of the two bedrooms in the back apartment and make it into a new bedroom for the house.

As an homage to the the tropics, Bianca Lanza had lavished bright color on the walls of all her previous homes. In this house, color was remedial: while she was undergoing chemotherapy, the brilliant walls answered her need "to feel happy." Ultimately, they also turned out to be a professional asset, providing a dramatic backdrop for the works of art she sells at special dinner parties and occasional private appointments. The vivid hues not only electrify the atmosphere, but enhance the artworks' presentation.

PRECEDING PAGES The sculpture above the mantel is by the Russian artist Leonid Sokov. The painting below it is by Lydia Rubio. **LEFT** The painting in the garden room is by Michael Abrams. **RIGHT** Lanza calls her bed the cocoon.

The walls were so beckoning that, at one point, Lanza had hundreds of works displayed. When she found she needed more focus and tranquillity to deal with her illness, she calmed things down by removing three-quarters of the pieces. New balance was achieved with dynamic result.

LEFT The "smoking chairs" are French Art Deco. **ABOVE** A collection of Italian ex votos. The one at center is Mexican.

MONTOYA
APARTMENT

The sumptuous congregation of
furnishings and art that fill Juan
Montoya's pied-à-terre unquestionably
indicates arrival—the mystery is
where. A *luxe* safari camp or a
jubilant agora? Perhaps a
Caribbean Casablanca?

A collection of African artifacts,
accessories, and textural references

combine with a hyperlinear composition—waves, zebra patterns, umbrella stripes—to create the apartment's exotic sense of animation.

Located in the Helen Mar, an Art Deco landmark on Indian Creek, the 1500-square-foot apartment was originally an undistinguished conversion of two adjacent studios. One became the living/dining area and the other the master bedroom, with the kitchen in between. A swivel panel of dark-stained wood lattice allows the kitchen and living room to be open or closed to each other, depending on the style of entertaining. Bamboo poles, installed to hold the pleated cotton-and-linen curtains that brush the floor, emphasize the apartment's only architectural asset—high ceilings.

The "civilized safari" ambience extends to the bedroom, whose walls are curtained, tentlike, in white and whose floors are covered with thick sisal. In the adjoining bathroom, Montoya converted a passenger train's overhead luggage racks into shelving, continuing the fantasy that this safari destination would be reached, of course, on the Orient Express.

PRECEDING PAGES The bright yellow Art Deco chairs are circa 1925. The printed zebra fabric covering the table is of Montoya's own design. **RIGHT** Hammock fabric covers mahogany chairs designed by Montoya. **OVERLEAF, LEFT** Leather masks from Ivory Coast and a carved bird from the Philippines are displayed on an African bench. **OVERLEAF, RIGHT** Montoya added the copper patinated circle to the nineteenth-century Chinese chest.

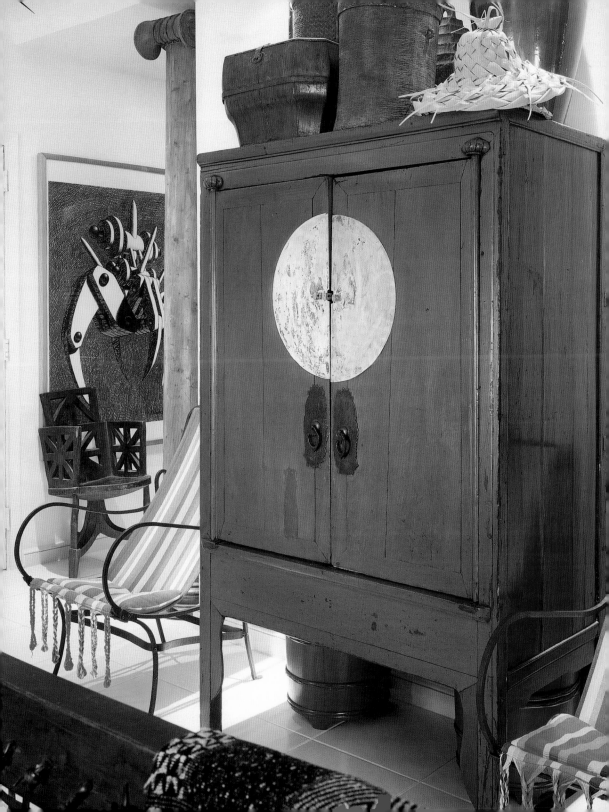

PRECEDING PAGES, LEFT Glass and wood windows are Turkish, seventeenth century. **PRECEDING PAGES, RIGHT** The African wall art is a wood and bone piece used for husking grain. **TOP** Mesh shelves for the compact bathroom come from a train car. **RIGHT** Italian bed linen is by Frette.

LOCSIN
APARTMENT

Architect Mario Locsin wanted a home filled with references to places he has lived, primarily his native Philippines. Since those islands share the climate and botany of South Beach, Locsin drew colors and objects into his apartment that represent his memories of other homes in New York, Madrid, and

PRECEDING PAGES Uninterrupted spatial flow enlarges the feel of the apartment. **LEFT** The dining table is from Knoll and the high ladderback chairs from the Hancock Shakers. The wall-sized photograph of the famous 1950s model Dovima is by Richard Avedon. **ABOVE** The framed renderings are from a 1940s architectural catalogue on brass and railings.

269

ABOVE A Portuguese tapestry found in Spain imparts a European flavor. **RIGHT** The remodeled kitchen was originally dark and enclosed. Built-in shelves and niches add places for display.

San Diego. "I wanted the spacious feel of a Soho loft with a slight Mediterranean sensation," he explains.

Against a backdrop of gray-green, pale golden ochre, and burnt khaki, Locsin has composed virtual "altars to time and serenity." His collection of period timepieces is displayed in concert with a collection of carved Philippino santos. Exquisite framed renderings from an architectural catalogue are symmetrically poised along a dining room wall. A carved wood segment of an archbishop's canopy is mounted and lighted with cathedral-like drama.

The ecclesiastical ambience reflects Locsin's specialization in liturgical design. Following a childhood as an altar boy, he studied theology along with architecture and art. The South Beach home he has created for himself is as timeless in its appeal as the spirits it evokes.

The bougainvillea growing along Locsin's balcony inspired the use of fuchsia and magenta accents inside.

CASA DE LUZ

When pioneer Miami Beach
architect Russell Pancoast designed
this expansive home on Biscayne
Bay in 1932, he named it Casa de
Luz for the unending shower of
light that filters through its rooms
and gardens. Its present owners
responded to that same luminosity
when they purchased it in 1994.

   The Spanish Mediterranean style
of architecture was common
among houses built in Miami and

PRECEDING PAGES A late-1800s Italian carved wood chest dominates the loggia. **ABOVE AND RIGHT** The original wrought-iron work includes subtropical garden scenes. **OVERLEAF** The living room is furnished with rugs, drapes, and upholstery fabrics from Monica James and Company. The Knole sofa, by Georges Smith, is covered in Burger linen velvet.

Miami Beach during the 1930s. "The minute I walked through the door into that loggia, I knew the house was for me," says the owner, who owns Monica James and Company, a home furnishings store in the Miami design district. A connoisseur of old world European design, she was swept away by the house's architectural richness: its arches, moldings, painted ceilings, wrought-iron fixtures and drapery hardware, not to mention the original chandeliers in the living and dining rooms. In fact, she found the setting so romantically beautiful that she and her husband held their wedding in the loggia, its poles wrapped with lilacs and gardenias.

Miami designer Fernando Sanchez collaborated on the design of the living room, garden, and loggia. His imprint is a distinctive colonial or "Guatemalan plantation" style.

Detail of a whitewashed eighteenth-century Louis XIV–style armchair bought in Paris.

ABOVE A sconce made from a vintage fixture with handcrafted shade and glass beads is by Kathleen Caid. **RIGHT** Dining room chairs are covered in Lee Jofa velvet. The mirror is from the Adam period. The hand-blocked, hand-stenciled, and hand-colored drapery fabric was designed for Andrew Lloyd Weber's music room and was made by Robert Kime of London. **OVERLEAF** The settee in the master bedroom sitting room was purchased from the Pillsbury estate in Palm Beach. Cushions are covered in Aubusson. The lamp is by Kathleen Caid. **PAGES 288–89** The garden room is furnished with McGuire rattan chairs upholstered in linen by Lee Jofa. The cabinet at right is a Palecek reproduction rattan from Indonesia.

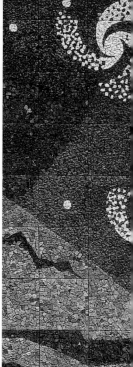

MURALS

The mural lives large as an art form on South Beach—figurative, abstract, painted, and mosaic. At far left are two murals by Michael Graves in the porte cochere of 1500 Ocean Drive, a condominum the architect designed. At top left is a mosaic that decorates the walls of a building that was once a theater, located south of Lincoln Road on Pennsylvania Avenue. At bottom left is an acrylic-on-canvas mural in the Banana Republic store at 800 Collins Avenue by artist Andrew Reid-Shep, 1995–96.

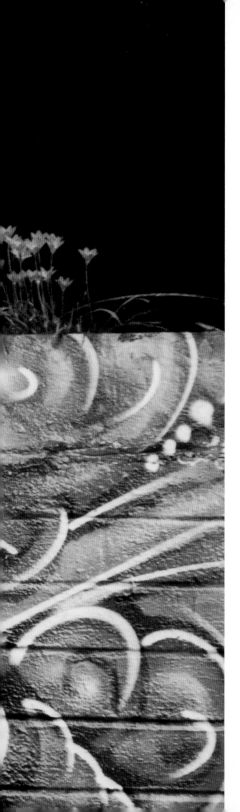

Murals painted by South Beach artist Jona Cerwinske, who is known for his monumental exterior wall murals and widely collected canvases. **ABOVE** A detail from a thatched-roof hut Cerwinske painted at Penrod's, the fish detail by Marcus Suarez. **LEFT** A residential garden wall. Photographs by Bianca Black.

hile the botany of South Beach is a splendor rich in color and exaggerated form, it is the skies that most surprise. Their vast changeability, their shocking hues and dramatic cloud formations are a perpetual command performance.

The homes in this chapter are subdued in inner expression to allow for a greater experience of the subtropical vista. Airy, light, and elegant, these houses are modernist in their openness, emphatic in their architectural simplicity. They are designed not to draw attention to inner drama, but as showcases for the theater of the sky and surroundings.

5

Homes:
Light and
Elegant

YABU-PUSHELBERG HOUSE

Toronto architects Glenn Pushelberg and George Yabu were looking for a pied-à-terre in the sun. They chose South Beach for its location because "it has texture, history, and is pedestrian—elements most American cities don't have." The architectural style they chose, on the other hand, is universal—as

pure an example of modern classicism as it is possible to design.

The original three-bedroom, two-bath house was built in 1953, a boxy amalgamation of rooms on a fairly contained lot. Pushelberg and Yabu, determined to open up the house to the light, installed glass doors across its rear façade. They chose terrazzo floors composed of aggregate so fine it looks almost like beach sand. Finally, they added a small courtyard entry for privacy and to filter the sun.

Furnishings came primarily from local venues—antique stores and the annual Miami Modernism show. A few Toronto and New York pieces have found their way into the rooms, but only those that reiterate the indoor/outdoor sensibility of the cool white interior. Its Corbusian starkness is reflected in the silence of the rooms, designed to be filled as easily with meditation as with frivolity.

PRECEDING PAGES Hurricane-resistant glass doors allow for a perpetual infusion of light. The three cottonwood stools in the corner are by Dan Pollack. **LEFT** The Grasshopper Chair by Eero Saarinen, circa 1948, was chosen for its sculptural quality. Beside it is a wooden bar by Gio Ponti. **OVERLEAF** The kitchen was completely renovated. The 1970s bar stools are by Joe Colombo.

LEFT The dining room table is illuminated by a surgical lamp from an operating room. **ABOVE** A contemporary Japanese chest in wood. **OVERLEAF** Behind the bed is an antique Japanese gate. **PAGES 306–7** The standing lamp is a classic design by Isamu Noguchi.

ABOVE Corner glass fenestration enhances the abundance of light in the master bedroom. The white ottoman is midcentury. **RIGHT** Jielde wall lamps are from France.

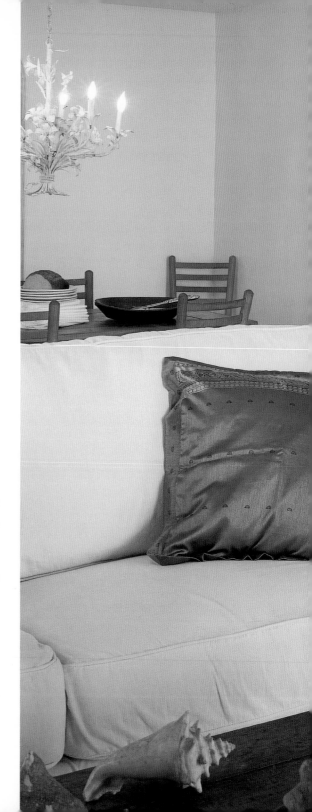

LEWIS
APARTMENT

Interior designer Sharon Lewis
divides her time between New York
and Miami Beach. Her soul, she says,
is "near the ocean," and so her pied-
à-terre is an homage to subtropical
calm. She painted the wood floors a
Caribbean blue, a color she later
found prevalent in another island
city, Key West. "I now call the color
'Key West blue,'" she confides. "It

immediately conveys a soothing, island feel."

Despite the obvious femininity of her home, Lewis likes its style because "it's not fancy or frilly." She filled it with pieces that relate her love of simplicity, yet are tinged with memory. The effect: poetry.

PAGE 310 Lewis's balcony overlooks the South Beach skyline. **PRECEDING PAGES** The wood table was made by a religious sect called the Nemish that uses more sophisticated tools than their purist brethren, the Amish. The white wood cabinet was found at a New York flea market. The television is inside. The white canvas slipcovers are by Cisco Brothers, California. **LEFT** The rustic sensibility of the kitchen was achieved by installing wainscoating, baseboards, and appropriate cabinet hardware, and with displays of hand-painted photography. 315

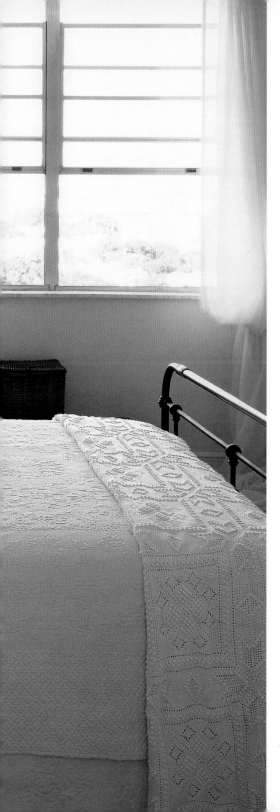

The bedroom is a study of white on white. The bed is
late nineteenth-century iron.

317

MUNCK
APARTMENT

As with most artists, quality of light
is a prime consideration for Paula
Munck, an illustrator who both lives
and works in her apartment high
above the Venetian causeway. From
dawn through dusk, her rooms are
filled with light reflecting off
Biscayne Bay and pouring in from
the western sky. The broad views

PRECEDING PAGES The Matisse-like illustration is by Munck, as is the cover design of the book lying on the sculpture stand at left. **ABOVE** Munck's designs appear on her dinnerware and in the framed picture on the wall. **RIGHT** An Isamu Noguchi floor lamp takes pride of place in the living room.

also take in a parade of sailboats and cruise ships.

Munck chose a pure palette of white for her walls and surfaces. Her home's only decorative distraction from the light and views is the generous presentation of her artwork—fanciful linear designs evocative of Matisse and Picasso that appear in prints on her walls, patterns on her dinnerware and ceramic pieces, and as cover designs on her numerous book projects.

Room-sized sisal rugs cover the floor, their neutral color appropriately unemphatic and a perfect complement to the blond wood of the vintage Heywood-Wakefield dining furniture. The sisal's natural fiber composition subtly reiterates the subtropical environment.

Munck's desk is Heywood-Wakefield. The view overlooks Biscayne Bay and downtown Miami.

MONTIFIORE
HOUSE

When Stephen Montifiore and Victoria DiNardo first purchased this modernist showcase, the bay-front house revealed little of its expansive character or pristine promise. Obscured beneath a façade of Mediterranean-style trappings, the modernist house, built in 1951, was a rambling conjunction of rooms that obscured their architectural and aesthetic beauty. The owners,

undaunted by the scope of their task, undertook the transformation with both purpose and pleasure, hiring New York–based designer Glenn Heim to restore the house's purist foundation.

Heim opened up the interior to space and light and "cleaned its lines." He demolished a low back porch enclosed with pillars and redesigned and rebuilt it to express "the forward movement of the period."

The purity of the architecture allows Montifiore and DiNardo great license in showcasing their collections of fantastical *objets d'art*. He collects 1950s clocks, she 1950s plastic handbags, and together they indulge a more than decade-long passion for art glass. The color and whimsicality of the collections is also reflected in their furniture—pieces that were avant-garde for their time and remain timeless as modern icons.

PRECEDING PAGES In the living room are a blue Corona chair, 1961, Danish, by Poul Volther, and a blue leather Charles sofa, designed by Antonio Citterio for B & B Italia. **LEFT** A chair by Gaetano Pesce from his 1970s Up series. The sculpture behind it is *Dufus,* 1988, Peter Reginato. **OVERLEAF** Venini Murano glass from the 1950s and 1960s. **PAGES 330–31** The collection on the left includes Russel Wright aluminum pieces and Italian glass from the 1950s. On the right are plastic handbags from the 1950s. **PAGES 332–33** The clocks are by Irving Harper for George Nelson, 1950s. The kitchen chairs are by Fornasetti.

PAGES 334–35 The Marshmallow sofa is by George Nelson. Easy Edges cardboard furniture is by Frank Gehry. **PAGES 336–37** The living room looks out toward the pool and pool house. **RIGHT** Designer Glenn Heim custom-designed the chaise longue in Sumbrella fabric with brushed stainless steel legs. **OVERLEAF** The sweeping overhang of the terrace replaces the original dark, pillared porch.

LIFEGUARD LOOKOUTS

The creator of these fanciful lifeguard stations, South Beach architect William Lane, sought inspiration for their design from toys, amusement parks, airport watchtowers, and mobile refreshment stands from the 1950s.

His invention perfectly marries nobility of mission with whimsy. What could be more appropriate for one of America's most popular resorts than lifeguard lookouts that seem to have sprung from a playground?

A s a city set on a man-made island and sprung from the clean angularity of the Art Deco style, South Beach is an illustration of nature's baroque tendency made rectilinear. The original South Beach garden was treated as an extension of the architecture, its botanical vocabulary imported and then mixed and matched for pure effect. From the beginning, the South Beach garden has been a quintessentially twentieth-century exercise in human dominance over nature.

Today florid spears of heliconia and ginger spike out from the earth; crotons and caladia mass like serrated canvases of speckled and striped paint; and palms of every variety pose in chorus line–like allées along the boulevards. Such plants as ficus and philodendron, seen only indoors in the North and Midwest, grow here to towering proportions. Ficus, popular for hedges, is shaped into living garden walls. Spiky dracena, heart-shaped pothos, and waxy-leaved peperomia all flourish in size and expanse.

6

Gardens
Courtyards
Pools

GARDENS

MONTIFIORE
HOUSE

The strong character of the
Montifiore garden belies its origin
as a tract of pavers and desolate
plantings. A static line of palm trees
and a Hong Kong orchid tree were
its few signs of botanical interest.
A pile of bright yellow boulders,
stacked one on top of the other,
commanded the focus at the front
of the house.

Victoria DiNardo and Stephen Montifiore, coming from New York, knew little about subtropical landscape design. Not long after moving in, Victoria came across a magazine story on a garden designed by Miami/Key West landscape architect Raymond Jungles. Its modern look appealed to her, as did his specific use of plants and color. Jungles, a disciple of the famed Brazilian landscape architect Roberto Burle Marx, spent nine months on the garden's transformation. He applied a predominantly green palette with accents of purple and white and added flowering trees, shade trees, numerous varieties of palms, and an abundance of bromeliads. Jungles also added a pond, a poured cement bridge, and beds of river rocks. From brutal dispassion, the Montifiore garden has grown into a world of sumptuous variety.

PRECEDING PAGES Landscape architect Raymond Jungles created a pond in what was previously the driveway. The bridge is poured concrete dyed with minerals. The stepping stones are poured concrete textured with salt. **RIGHT** The stones are black Mexican river rocks. **OVERLEAF** The thorny-trunked succulent "tree" in the foreground is a pachypodium.

CASA DE LUZ

The color and careful cultivation of this bay-front garden was introduced by its present owners. Originally, the garden was far more tropical and overgrown, hosting thousands of orchids and bromeliads. In fact, its previous owner once flew in a 727 jet filled with orchids from Venezuela.

Today, dense with flowering vegetation, the garden's character has been both subdued by the addition of brick paths and a lily pond, and enlivened by the bright contrast of color and form.

PAGES 352–53 Brick pavers and tiles lead through the dense growth of the garden. Their rustic beauty suitably complements that of the new garden design. **PRECEDING PAGES, LEFT** A wall of ferns animates the Mediterranean-style fountain. **PRECEDING PAGES, RIGHT** The present owners added the lily pond and brick paths. **LEFT** The expansive overhang of the loggia allows for abundant shade and air circulation.

LIPSCHUTZ
HOUSE

In the early 1990s, when Suzanne
Lipschutz purchased her 1926
Mediterranean-style house in the
heart of South Beach, it was
surrounded by little more than
lawn, front and back. She gave
the two nondescript shrubs that
languished on the bare tract to a
neighbor—in effect, cleansing the
botanical palette.

Lipschutz is a New Yorker and the owner of Manhattan's Secondhand Rose, a store specializing in late nineteenth-century avant-garde decorative arts. She knew next to nothing about subtropical gardening. And because the house serves only as a weekend or vacation home, her attentions to the landscape were, by nature, erratic. Nevertheless, she was determined to create a dense, self-sustaining wonderland.

To deconstruct the lawn, Lipschutz applied layers of newspaper—the *New York Times,* of course—and mulch over the grass "until it simply gave up." Then, on each visit to South Beach, she would buy "a hundred plants a day wherever I went, little tiny things just to see how they would exist on their own." Her sources ranged from "fabulous growers in Homestead and others who specialize in exotics" to garage sales and the Home Depot nursery.

The garden palette originated with musas— the botanical family that includes bananas, travelers "palms," and heliconias. Numerous trees then came from a gardeners' flea market, and soon the landscape was replete with all varieties of palms: triangle palms, bottle palms, pigmy date palms, oil palms (the largest variety in the world), and, of course, this being Florida, coconut palms.

PRECEDING PAGES The now dense landscape replaces a lawn that was all but bare of vegetation. **LEFT** A flowering travelers palm.

ABOVE The stripes of flowering ginger leaves contrast with those of the languid palm. **RIGHT** Philodendron vine grows to vast size. **OVERLEAF** Wrought-iron entry gates in Chinese red contrast with the intense green of the foliage, left, as does the stand of magenta coleus, right.

Lipschutz rearranged plants the way many homeowners move furniture—or the way an artist composes and recomposes a canvas. With time came density, and with density, wonderment—at the beauty and durability of the garden. Throughout the cultivation, Lipschutz adhered to her self-defined creed regarding care and maintenance. "I water a plant regularly for two weeks; after that, it's on its own."

LEFT A travelers palm at top left towers over a flowering pink hibiscus. **OVERLEAF, LEFT** Botanical shadows and silhouettes pattern the deep coloration of the house. **OVERLEAF, RIGHT** Detail of a triangle palm.

PRECEDING PAGES A stand of banana trees. **LEFT** A confluence of botanical and man-made ornaments. **OVERLEAF** A triangle palm in full expanse.

373

COURTYARDS AND DETAILS

It is both the large picture and the small—the public courtyard and the precise detail—that account for the variety in South Beach gardens. As in most urban environments, a courtyard garden is coveted. "Common grounds," around which social life revolved in the decades before air-conditioning

PAGES 376–77 A public courtyard garden beautifies Washington Avenue between 10th and 11th Streets. **PRECEDING PAGES, LEFT** An entry courtyard with applied pilasters in a Mediterranean-style house. **PRECEDING PAGES, RIGHT** Barry Zaid created a courtyard garden where originally there was no more than a concrete slab. **LEFT** The entrance terrace of the Delano is animated by an unexpected play of scale.

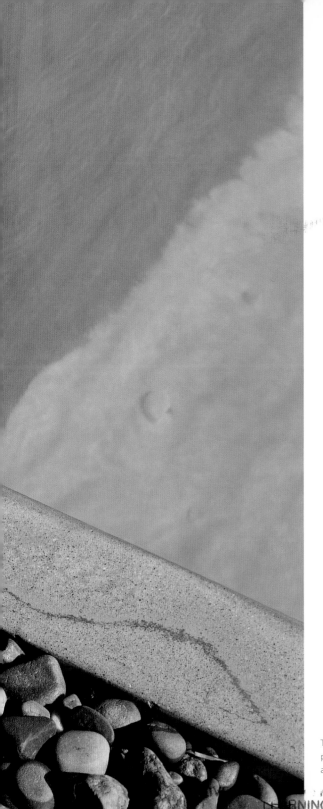

The pebbled border around the Yabu-Pushelberg
pool is Japanese in aesthetic effect. It functions as
a reservoir for water that spills over the edge.   **383**

and television, provided for convenient congregation as well as relief from the airless heat of small apartments. In fact, many buildings were sited around common courtyards specifically to maximize the number of windows through which air could circulate. Endless hours of conversation and countless games of mahjong and pinochle once filled the life of these settings. Today the private courtyard is prized for entertaining and gardening, and the public courtyard for socializing and relaxation.

Regardless of a garden's size or style, it is the details that enrich, or even establish, its character. A color, a texture, a pattern, an ornament—each provides a visual punctuation or focus to the overall form of the landscape.

The textured geometry of bamboo leaves, fallen into a cross-hatch pattern over a grid of pampass grass clumps, is a feature of the entrance courtyard.

The filigree of the Victorian wrought-iron
furniture makes for dramatic contrast with
the bold jungle of the Leddick garden.

The stairway leading up to the Leddick house is tiled in the Mediterranean style of Palm Beach architect Addison Mizner, with each riser decorated in a different pattern.

POOLS

An oasis is not a true oasis without water—cooling, calming, refreshing. A pool is the ultimate invitation to leisure, whether floating somnambulently or splashing at play, whether contemplating reflection or swimming for simple pleasure. Like its homes and gardens, South Beach pools take many forms—sunny and glamorous, shady and intimate, playful and dramatic.

So intrinsic is the pool to the South Florida way of living that even its intimation refreshes a garden setting: when the Canadian artist Charles Pachter took a vacation home in South Beach, he had neither the time nor the interest to maintain a pool. But the idea of a pool in his backyard was too compelling to ignore. Pachter did what any true artist would—he painted one.

PRECEDING PAGES A pair of columns creates a formal pool setting. **RIGHT** In Charles Pachter's trompe l'oeil pool, neither the water nor the tiles are real. Photograph by Charles Pachter. **OVERLEAF** The Montifiore pool. **PAGES 396–97** The Delano hotel pool.

SOURCES

The Bass Museum
2100 Washington Avenue
Miami Beach, FL 33139
305/673-7166

Steven Brooke, Photographer
7910 S.W. 54th Court
Miami, FL 33143
305/667-8075
smbrooke@aol.com

Jona Cerwinske, Graphic Design, Murals,
and Fine Art
Miami Beach, FL 33139
305/604-0484

DACRA Development
1632 Pennsylvania Avenue
Miami Beach, FL 33139
305/531-8700

Delano
1685 Collins Avenue
Miami Beach, FL 33139
305/672-3000

The Hotel
801 Collins Avenue
Miami Beach, FL 33139
305/531-2222

The Impala
1228 Collins Avenue
Miami Beach, FL 33139
305/673-2021

Indian Creek Hotel
2727 Indian Creeek Drive
Miami Beach, FL 33140
305/531-2727

Raymond Jungles ASLA
517 Duval Street, #206
Key West, FL 33140
305/294-6700

Bianca Lanza, Interior Designer, Art Dealer
Miami Beach, FL 33139
305/801-3669
aibart811@aol.com

Sharon Lewis, Interior Designer
214 East 83rd Street
New York, NY 10028
212/535-0989

Locsin Design
1611 West Avenue
Miami Beach, FL 33139
305/531-9003

Ruth Marten, Illustrator/Artist
8 West 13th Street, #7RW
New York, NY 10011
212/645-0233

The Mermaid
354 Washington Avenue
Miami Beach, FL 33139
305/538-5324

Monica James and Company
140 N.E. 40th Street
Miami, FL 33137
305/576-6222

William Lane, AIA
350 Lincoln Road, #501
Miami Beach, FL 33139
305/531-5292

Juan Montoya Interior Design
330 East 59th Street
New York, NY 10022
212/421-2400

Paula Munck, Designer
115 Third San Marino Terrace
Miiami Beach, FL 33139
305/535-6577
pmunck@aol.com

Pearl
1 Ocean Drive
Miami Beach, FL 33139
305/673-1575

The Scull Sisters
305/532-0417

Tap-Tap
819 Fifth Street
Miami Beach, FL 33139
305/672-2898

The Tides
1320 Ocean Drive
Miami Beach, FL 33139
305/604-5070

The Wolfsonian
1001 Washington Avenue
Miami Beach, FL 33139
305/531-1001

Yabu-Pushelberg Architects
55 Booth Avenue
Toronto M4M 2M3, Ontario Canada
416/778-9779

Barry Zaid, Designer
752 Meridian Avenue
Miami Beach, FL 33139
305/531-1277
bzaid@bellsouth.net

Bernard Zyscovich, AIA
100 N. Biscayne Boulevard
Miami, FL 33132
305/372-5222
www.zyscovich.com

OVERLEAF The reception desk at the
Indian Creek Hotel.